THE FOUR VILLAINS OF CLINICAL TRIAL AGREEMENT DELAYS AND HOW TO DEFEAT THEM

Addressing CTA Delays Comprehensively

DÉBORA S. ARAUJO
FOREWORD BY T. J. SHARPE

Copyright © 2018 Débora S. Araujo.

All rights reserved. No part of this book may be used or reproduced by any means, graphic, electronic, or mechanical, including photocopying, recording, taping or by any information storage retrieval system without the written permission of the author except in the case of brief quotations embodied in critical articles and reviews.

WestBow Press books may be ordered through booksellers or by contacting:

WestBow Press
A Division of Thomas Nelson & Zondervan
1663 Liberty Drive
Bloomington, IN 47403
www.westbowpress.com
1 (866) 928-1240

Because of the dynamic nature of the Internet, any web addresses or links contained in this book may have changed since publication and may no longer be valid. The views expressed in this work are solely those of the author and do not necessarily reflect the views of the publisher, and the publisher hereby disclaims any responsibility for them.

Any people depicted in stock imagery provided by Getty Images are models, and such images are being used for illustrative purposes only.
Certain stock imagery © Getty Images.

ISBN: 978-1-9736-2269-7 (sc)
ISBN: 978-1-9736-2268-0 (e)

Library of Congress Control Number: 2018903183

Print information available on the last page.

WestBow Press rev. date: 04/06/2018

CONTENTS

Foreword by T. J. Sharpe vii
Acknowledgments ix
Introduction xi

Chapter 1: Villain #1: The Numeror—Ineffective Site-Budget
    Negotiations 1
Chapter 2: Villain #2: Middleman Malaise—Poor Outsourced
    Negotiations 10
Chapter 3: Villain #3: Adoptaphobia And Innovaphobia Syndrome—
    Lack of Industry Adoption and Innovation 18
Chapter 4: Villain #4: Mr. Peripheral—All the Other Things Affecting
    CTA Negotiations 35
Chapter 5: CTA Delays Symptom Checker 46

Appendix A: Streamlining CTA Negotiations Checklist 53
Appendix B: CLEAR™ (Common Language Evaluation and
    Reconciliation) 57
Appendix C: Rest of World (ROW) General CTA Country
    Requirements 61

FOREWORD

When Débora S. Araujo pulled me aside at an industry conference, I had no idea just how involved she was in one of the most important areas of clinical research—getting a trial started. It is *the* one moment in a clinical trial when all stakeholders are on the same page, but getting there takes quite a bit of navigation, negotiation, and compromise.

After she mentioned she was putting the final touches on a new book, *The Four Villains of Clinical Trial Agreement Delays and How to Defeat Them*, she asked if I would write the foreword. I ecstatically agreed. As a blogger and a clinical trial advocate, I often get the chance to relay to the pharmaceutical and clinical research industry the ups and downs I faced in participating in two separate late-stage cancer trials. Nowhere would this story be more appropriate than to kick off a book that addresses the delays that myself and many other patients face in finding and enrolling in a trial.

When I was diagnosed in 2012 with stage IV melanoma, my first oncologist offered standard-of-care chemotherapy and a measly twenty-four-month prognosis. Determined to watch my family grow up—my son was only four weeks old at the time, and my daughter was just two years older—I looked for hope, which came in the form of clinical trials for new immunotherapies. That glimmer of hope was nearly dashed, along with my chance to participate in a potentially life-saving trial, when the execution of the clinical trial agreement (CTA) was continually delayed for more than a month.

Five years later, after telling my story at that industry conference, Débora followed my presentation with one of her own—on the four villains of clinical trial agreements. The timing couldn't have been more perfect. She was able to cite several examples used in the keynote while walking the audience through a subject that is not easy to digest.

Making legal documents captivating is certainly a challenge, but when a comic storyline like the "four villains" is intertwined with real-world examples, this book becomes more than just a series of chapters. Yes, you will learn about the pitfalls of the clinical trial agreement and strategies for addressing them. You will also get context on what happens when issues cause delays and push out the contract execution.

Estimated times for clinical trial agreement execution vary from ten to eighteen weeks, but even with an optimistic thirteen-week timeframe, that is still a full three months. In that quarter, 150,000 cancer patients will die; over 400,000 people will pass away from the top six disease-related causes of death. Countless others will suffer with serious, chronic, or untreated conditions.[1] Yet a piece of paper waiting to be signed will likely deny someone, somewhere, the chance to live a longer, healthier, or better life through a clinical trial.

With more than a decade of clinical trial experience, Débora has intimate knowledge of clinical contracts, budgets, and payment management. Having worked for and with multiple pharmaceutical sponsors and investigator sites, she utilizes her robust knowledge and experience to drive practical change in the industry via thought leadership material, presentations, and consulting engagements.

Readers will find a wealth of practical ways to improve clinical trial agreement negotiations and avoid delays from the sponsor, CRO, and investigator site sides. Additionally, you will see how tackling the "villains" of clinical trial agreement delays simultaneously can surpass the results they would have if tackling any one of them in isolation.

The Four Villains of Clinical Trial Agreement Delays and How to Defeat Them gives an animated view of navigating the real-world obstacles faced while kicking off a clinical trial through the CTA. I am honored to be able to provide the foreword for this endeavor, and I trust you will glean plenty of villain-crushing information from these pages. After all, there are patients out there who are waiting for a superhero to bring them a treatment to improve, extend, or even save their lives.

---

[1] "National Center for Health Statistics." Centers for Disease Control and Prevention. March 17, 2017. Accessed February 28, 2018. https://www.cdc.gov/nchs/fastats/leading-causes-of-death.htm

ACKNOWLEDGMENTS

This book is dedicated to my parents, Sobral and Elza. Thank you for all your years of selfless sacrifice, hard work, and loving prayers to give me a better opportunity in this life. I am eternally grateful for everything—I sincerely am.

To my husband, Altair, my best friend and the wind beneath my wings. Thank you for always being up for my crazy ideas and dreams. Thank you for all your encouragement and for helping me get out of my comfort zone. I love you.

To my sons, Matthew Brad and Timothy Brandon, my precious gifts from God. I love you, my boys. Being your mom is the greatest honor.

To everyone who has ever felt inapt to accomplish a certain dream or truly make a difference in this world, I dedicate this book to you. Just like the biblical story of David and Goliath, sometimes the "stones" in our hands may seem too small and insignificant to defeat certain giants in our lives. But sometimes being willing to pick up and throw those small stones is all that is needed for the impossible to happen. Don't delay. Go for it!

INTRODUCTION

Imagine with me for a moment you are your favorite superhero, charged with the task of saving the world from villains such as the Joker, Lex Luthor, Doctor Doom, and the Green Goblin. You would not be very effective—or much of a superhero, for that matter—if you only took one of them out while letting the others roam free. In the same way, as an industry, we cannot effectively tackle the issue of delays in the execution of clinical trial agreements (CTAs) by only addressing one or two of the "villains" contributing to this industry-wide problem.

In this book, we will explore the different villains who contribute to CTA negotiation delays and provide some practical ways to address each of them. By tackling the different factors contributing to this industry-wide issue concurrently, we can accelerate the change that we, as an industry, and our patients desperately need.

Lights, Camera, Action!

I know the topic of CTA negotiations may not be a sexy one for most people (except the few like me), yet it is one that can have an incredible impact in the lives of countless families. If you work day in and day out with CTA negotiations, you may not think of it as purposeful, life changing, or heroic. However, I challenge you to look beneath the surface to the compounded impact it can have for hundreds of thousands of patients and their families, both now and in the years to come. I further challenge you to see yourself as a type of superhero, charged each day with the mission of defeating the villains who could keep a dad from seeing his kid's next birthday, a family from sharing another holiday together, or a child from enjoying just being a kid with his friends for another summer.

It may seem like a bit of a stretch—maybe even somewhat idealistic—but if we don't see ourselves as existing to make a difference, to serve and solve a problem, what is the point of our lives? I believe, even in the world of CTAs, we can make a difference.

As my favorite superhero, Wonder Woman, said, "If it means interfering in an ensconced, outdated system to help just one woman, man, or child … I'm willing to accept the consequences"[2]

Let's do this.

---

[2] Wonder Women #170

CHAPTER 1

Villain #1: Ineffective Site-Budget Negotiations

Villain Name: THE NUMEROR

> There is a right and a wrong in the universe. And the distinction is not hard to make.
> —Superman

If you are involved in study start-up, you have likely seen many instances in which the sponsor/CRO and site have agreed on the legal language of the CTA only to experience delays due to the proposed budget. Following are some ways to effectively deal with this villain. Some approaches might be a better fit for certain organizations, and other approaches might be more appropriate for others. The important thing is to be aware that there are options today that can drastically improve site-budget negotiations for any organization. Let's explore a few of these.

How to Defeat This Villain

Provide Procedure-Level Budgets to Sites

Imagine for a moment that you are a contractor. A potential client comes to you and says he wants you to build a three thousand-square-foot, five-bedroom, three-bathroom house and will give you two hundred dollars for the entire project. After your initial instinct to tell him that he is out of his mind (or worse), your next reaction would likely be to ask him how he imagined two hundred dollars could cover all costs as well as what was included in his cost estimate.

In the same way, investigator sites are many times perplexed when they receive the sponsor's initial budget proposal containing sponsor expectations of what the study will cost to run from the site side. Sites are perplexed for two main reasons. First, the proposed budget usually does not match the actual costs of running the study at their site. (We will discuss this point later in the chapter.) And second, there is very little transparency into what the cost provided by the sponsor includes. This second point often happens when sponsors send a site budget only showing either a total per-visit or a total per-patient cost.

This makes it very challenging for sites to compare "apples to apples" what the sponsor is offering for each study's protocol-required procedure or task against their internal analysis of what it will cost. Instead, this issue can be easily addressed if the sponsor provides a budget proposal that links each protocol-required procedure or task to a specific cost.

I can almost hear the obvious objection to this approach: will this not further delay negotiations if negotiations will now be made at the procedure level? My honest answer from personal experience in various sponsors, site-side experience, and feedback from numerous colleagues in the industry is no. If the budget proposal sent to the site is built within fair market value costs and all the procedures and tasks required by the protocol's schedule of events table, there should not be a huge variation between the sponsor and site costs. If there is a huge discrepancy, then either the sponsor or the site is making incorrect assumptions that should be addressed and resolved in the process of the negotiation. A simple conference call between the parties can help clarify the root of any discrepancies. If an agreement is still not reached, then it may not be a good partnership to pursue. The point is that a certain level of transparency is the right foundation on which to build negotiations and should not be viewed as a bottleneck.

Tip

Sponsors can provide CTA documents, including the site budget, along with other required start-up documents prior to the prestudy visit. This will ensure sites have ample time to contrast the proposed budget against their internal coverage analysis and negotiate as needed without impacting regulatory document submissions. Many sites will not be able to submit internal regulatory documents without first going through CTA documents and negotiations.

Customize Budgets while Maintaining Fair Market Value

Many global sponsors and CROs develop one standard site budget for a country (some even use the same budget template for all countries) and send it out for site review without taking into consideration geographical locations, institution size, and other pertinent information. This increases the number of days sites will need to revise the budget proposal with more appropriate and site-specific numbers. It also increases the number of days required to obtain the necessary internal sponsor approvals to revise the budget items.

Starting out with a robust, accurate, and equitable site budget based on geographical location, institution size, and site intelligence can shrink the number of days needed for the back-and-forth among sponsor, CRO, and site. Sponsors should consider the differences in health-care costs among global geographical locations, even within a country. There are also industry tools and technologies that allow you, to a certain degree, to tailor the site budget to specific institutions.

Objections to this approach are usually rooted in the fear of not maintaining fair market value (FMV). To clarify, maintaining FMV while producing more accurate and robust site budgets can be achieved if the sponsor/CRO consistently applies a standard process and can show proper documentation to prove they have followed this process in the event of an audit.[3]

The key here is setting up an excellent initial structure to ensure a

---

[3] Goldfarb M., Norman. *"Journal of Clinical Research Best Practices"*, vol. 12 no. 8, (2016). https://firstclinical.com/journal/2016/1608_Budget_Negotiation.pdf

consistent process that is replicated for all sites while considering their unique differences. This is the foundation of maintaining FMV. This solution may require some time up front to build the infrastructure, but it will also prove to be amazingly effective in speeding up site-budget negotiations and defending FMV during an audit.

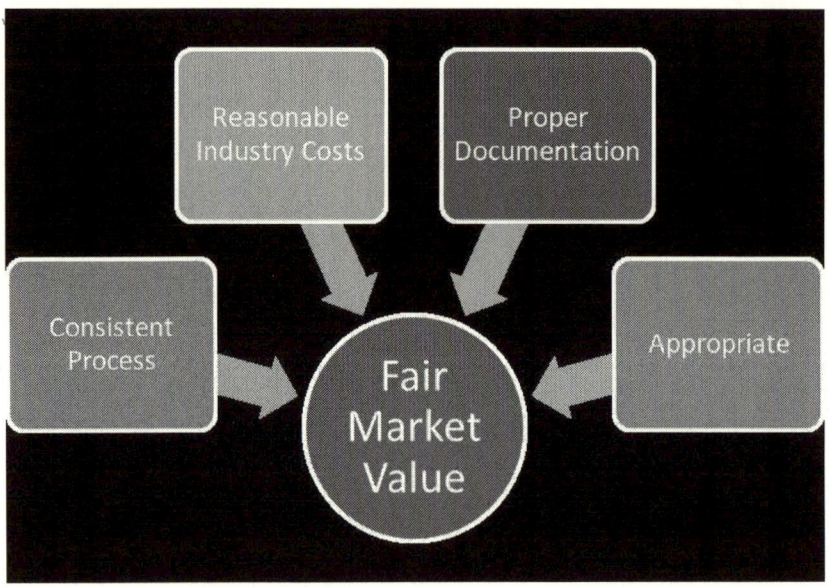

Why Is Fair Market Value (FMV) Important in CTA Negotiations?

The importance of the FMV topic can be traced back to a regulation published in 2003 by the Office of Inspector General (OIG). The regulation was titled "OIG Compliance Program Guidance for Pharmaceutical Manufacturers" and stipulated that payments for research services should be fair market value for legitimate, reasonable, and necessary services.[4] Unfortunately, regulators never provided clear guidelines on how exactly fair market value should be obtained. This has left both sponsors and sites in a tough spot; they still are required to abide by the regulation and can suffer steep fines for not doing so but have received no clear direction as to how to do this.

---

[4] Snyder, A. "Fair Market Value Conundrum: Solutions for Sponsors and Sites." Applied Clinical Trials Home. October 16, 2017. Accessed February 28, 2018. http://www.appliedclinicaltrialsonline.com/fair-market-value-conundrum-solutions-sponsors-and-sites?pageID=1.

FMV and the Real Estate Comparison

One of the important questions to ask when establishing and reviewing the market value of anything is this: "What are most reasonable people willing to pay for something comparable?" Think about how home appraisal values are established in real estate. An owner looking to sell a home may have installed gold chandeliers and heated marble floors, but if comparable homes (in size, number of rooms, and age) in the neighborhood are selling for $100,000, this home is likely to be appraised at a similar value despite what the owner believes it is worth. This is not to say that someone cannot offer to pay $1 million for this home. It simply means that the higher offer would be outside of the market value concept. In real estate, this is not common, but it is acceptable. Generally, the value of an item or service is determined by what the market is willing to pay for it. However, in the realm of clinical research, the word *fair* makes things more complicated.

The word *fair* takes the concept of market value a step further to include reasonableness, appropriateness, supporting documentation, and consistency, among other concepts. It is important to understand this difference to avoid a potential perception of bribery and impropriety when setting and negotiating study-site budgets. Remember that just because something is market value because someone is willing to pay a certain amount for it does not necessarily mean it is also fair market value.

FMV Question Checklist

- Is there a formal FMV process?
- Is the process well documented?
- Is the process applied consistently?
- Is the FMV process/approach perceived as reasonable?
- Is it easily defensible in an audit or other legal matter?
- Is it perceived as appropriate and ethical? Does it pass the classic newspaper test question? How would it look on the front page of tomorrow's newspaper (or newsfeed)?
- Is the market data value source methodical and logical in its determination of what is fair market value?

FMV Deviations Checklist

- Is there a formal process in place for deviations?
- Is the process well documented?
- Is the deviation consistently applied for exceptions?
- Is it perceived as reasonable?
- Is it defensible in an audit or legal case?
- Is it appropriate and perceived as ethical?

Additional Regulations and Guidance on Fair Market Value

Anti-Kickback Statute

The anti-kickback statute generally prohibits offering, paying, soliciting, or receiving remuneration to induce or reward referrals for items or services payable by government health-care programs, including Medicare and Medicaid.[5]

42 CFR §411.351

Fair market value means the value in arm's-length transactions, consistent with the general market value. "General market value" means the price that an asset would bring as the result of bona fide bargaining between well-informed buyers and sellers who are not otherwise in a position to generate business for the other party, or the compensation that would be included in a service agreement as the result of bona fide bargaining between well-informed parties to the agreement who are not otherwise in a position to generate business for the other party, on the date of acquisition of the asset or at the time of the service agreement.[6]

Sunshine Act and Open Payments

---

[5] Stanger, K. C. Stark Requirements for Physician Contracts. www.hhhealthlawblog.com. http://www.hhhealthlawblog.com/2014/12/stark-requirements-for-physician-contracts.html (Retrieved October 14, 2017)

[6] 42 CFR 411.351 - Definitions. (n.d.). www.law.cornell.edu. https://www.law.cornell.edu/cfr/text/42/411.351. (Retrieved October 07, 2017)

The Physician Payments Sunshine Act is part of the Affordable Care Act and requires that payments made by pharmaceutical and device companies to physicians and teaching hospitals be made available to the public through a searchable database. This program is overseen by the Centers for Medicare and Medicaid Services and is made available yearly on their website (CMS.gov). Payments include speaking fees, gifts, travel, research, and meals.[7]

Stark Law

Stark Law: "Entities that employ or contract with physicians must ensure their agreements are structured to comply with the federal Ethics in Patient Referrals Act ("Stark") if they intend to bill Medicare for services rendered or referred by the physicians."

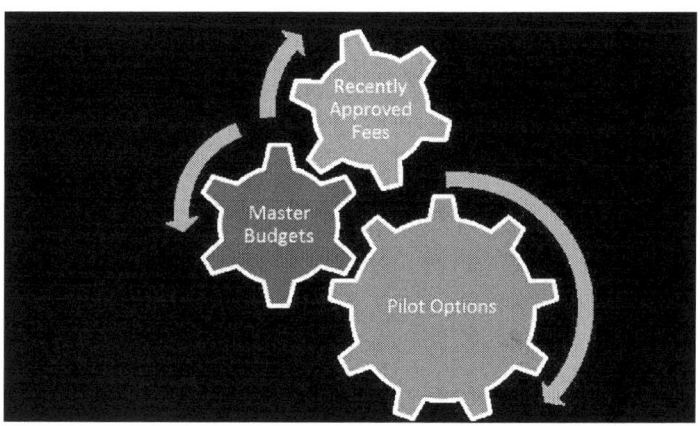

Negotiate Master Site Budgets

For those sites with which the sponsor has already negotiated master clinical trial agreements (CTAs), it may be beneficial to establish a master site budget as well. By coming to an agreement on certain routine costs and fees, the return on investment of that negotiation time may prove to be invaluable in expediting future trials with that site. This approach may be worth piloting with frequently used strategic partnerships and networks to test its effectiveness for your specific organization. The key here is that

---

[7] Open Payments. www.cms.gov. https://www.cms.gov/openpayments/ (Retrieved October 14, 2017).

both parties be willing to use the negotiated amounts for the established timeframe and not attempt to re-negotiate as this defies the purpose of such master negotiations. Nevertheless, if used appropriately by both parties it can streamline the process significantly.

Start with Previously Approved Fees

If a master site budget is not a possibility, and if workload permits, simply customizing each site's budget (using previously negotiated and agreed-upon costs) prior to distribution may slash negotiation time. Overhead, fixed fees, and other appropriate costs are many times not protocol specific; customization of these items can help start negotiations on a good note as well as reduce the back-and-forth. To be clear, this does not mean that a sponsor should provide the same site budget used for a previous study to the same site without regard for the current study protocol. This does mean that certain fixed and at times routine procedures can be proactively used when developing new site budgets for a new study after recent negotiations with the same site.

What Can Sites Do?
Justify Up Front

If you have any changes to the proposed sponsor budget, provide all justification documents for established site costs and fees up front and along with your revised costs. Don't wait until the sponsor or CRO contact requests these documents, as this back-and-forth only adds to the negotiation time. These justifications, when provided up front, will help the sponsor/CRO to review your changes against their internal policies and obtain any necessary internal approvals in parallel with the review of any other changes in the CTA document.

Site Budgets Checklist

- Provide procedure-level budgets to investigator sites (sponsor).
- Customize site budgets within formal fair market value (FMV) process (sponsor).
- Have and use fair market value (FMV) process that is (sponsor and site)
    - ○ formal,
    - ○ well documented,
    - ○ consistently applied,
    - ○ reasonable,
    - ○ defensible,
    - ○ passes the ethical test, and
    - ○ has a methodical and logical market data value source.
- Have and use a fair market value (FMV) deviation process that is (sponsor and site)
    - ○ formal
    - ○ well documented
    - ○ consistently applied for exceptions
    - ○ reasonable
    - ○ defensible and
    - ○ passes the ethical test.
- Explore if master-budget negotiations are appropriate (sponsor and site).
- Explore using recently approved fees at the start of negotiations (sponsor).
- Provide justification documents up front in negotiation process (site).

CHAPTER 2

Villain #2: Poor Outsourced Negotiations
Villain Name: MIDDLEMAN MALAISE

> With great power comes great responsibility.
> —Spiderman

The right CRO or functional service provider (FSP) can be an excellent and strategic partner in helping sponsors have a wider and farther reach. This is no different when it comes to CRO-managed CTA negotiations. The CRO/FSP is an extension of the sponsor's brand and reputation. However, CRO-managed negotiations still require a level of sponsor guidance and oversight. At times, some sponsors have viewed CRO-outsourced work as something for which they no longer need to provide oversight. This is a huge mistake that can cause weeks of CTA delays and damage the sponsor's relationship with the site. It is vital that sponsors develop, execute, and train on an appropriate oversight strategy for all outsourced work, including CTA negotiations, and apply it consistently. Let's explore a few options for how to defeat this villain.

How to Defeat This Villain

Leverage Existing Master CTAs

A concern that sites continue to voice is the experience they continually have with some CROs regarding existing master CTAs between the site and the sponsor. The frustration occurs when a master CTA is already in place between the sponsor and site—yet attempts are made by the CRO to use a CRO-specific contract. There is no reason to start from scratch in a CTA negotiation when the site and sponsor already have a master CTA in place. This is a contractual agreement that needs to be honored and leveraged. It is extremely discouraging to sites to have invested time in negotiating a master CTA only to not have it be used. Sponsors can help by discussing early on with the selected CRO how the current master agreements between the sponsor and the sites will be leveraged and used for the current outsourced study. This simple conversation can speed up negotiations by weeks for the affected sites.

Provide Clear Communication Pathway to Sponsor

Of course, the purpose of outsourcing work to a CRO/FSP is that the CRO/FSP is compensated for performing the tasks for which the sponsor is typically responsible. This often includes CTA negotiations. However, the sponsor is the one with the most skin in the game, remains ultimately responsible for the clinical trial, and will be most benefitted or hurt by the relationship with and performance of the selected investigator sites. It is in the sponsor's best interest to make sure a good relationship with sites is established early in the study start-up process, even if a CRO/FSP will be negotiating the budgets and contracts and conducting the trial.

This can be done by providing selected sites with a specific contact at the sponsor for escalation of major concerns or issues during the negotiation process. It needs to be clear to sites that the CRO/FSP is conducting negotiations on the sponsor's behalf—but that the relationship with the site is important enough for the sponsor to be involved and available. The study start-up process, including CTA negotiations, is one of the first interactions sites will have with sponsors even if through a CRO/FSP. If trust and a good relationship are not established, then difficulties are likely from that point on.

Address CRO Staff Turnover and Level of Experience

One frequent piece of feedback from sites regarding sources of delay in CTA negotiations for outsourced studies is the issue of CRO staff turnover.

The issue is not the turnover itself, but rather the quality of the transition for ongoing negotiations within the CRO. Weeks can be wasted while sites try to identify a new CRO contact who can resolve the open issues and resume negotiations if the original CRO contact suddenly leaves the organization. Many times, the knowledge and progress gained through weeks of negotiations can be lost with the turnover if there is not an effective transition plan in place. This issue can be prevented, or at least minimized, by discussing and planning for resource transitions during contract negotiations between sponsor and CRO, as well as during CRO-oversight discussions.

A second concern within this topic is the level of experience of the CRO contract negotiators. Sponsors will frequently ask for confirmation of the appropriate level of experience of CRO project directors, managers, and CRAs. However, the level of experience for CRO contract negotiators is almost never discussed. During times of CRO staff turnover, this can lead to the assignment of very junior CRO staff with very little negotiation experience who lack the understanding needed for CTA negotiations. In turn, this can add weeks (and aggravation) to the negotiation process. Negotiators with strong technical experience as well as good soft skills possess golden characteristics that make CTA negotiations flow smoother.

Outsourcing CTA Negotiations Wisely

While there is not one single model that works for every situation, if a sponsor does decide to outsource the CTA negotiation piece of their study start-up, then ensuring the use of the right CRO/FSP is critical. Less experienced sponsors may believe that if all the pieces of a study are fully outsourced to a major CRO, then efficiencies will be gained in each separate task or deliverable. Unfortunately, this has not always been proven true.

It has been my experience that the best outcomes for the operational management of a trial come from ensuring each major task has the right, fit-for-purpose talent, technology, and model—specifically during study start-up. Sponsors should analyze their individual organization's structure, culture, objectives, and talent prior to deciding what type of model to use for CTA negotiations (either in-house or outsourced models). It is possible to have an efficient in-house model for one region of the world and an efficient outsourced model for another. The important thing is selecting a model that is fit for its purpose. If an outsourced model is selected, sponsors then have the even more important duty of selecting the one CRO/FSP who will truly drive CTA negotiations forward.

If a choice is available, hire subject matter experts for CTA negotiations. Utilize either expert in-house staff or niche outsourced vendors whose expertise is focused on CTA negotiations. Don't employ a jack-of-all-trades to handle CTA negotiations and expect negotiations to be done efficiently, thoroughly, or with high quality. It can result in hit-or-miss negotiations. Study start-up is too important to delegate to inexperienced entities and hope it gets done right.

Selecting the Right CRO for CTA Negotiations

When the opportunity arises to choose from the pool of CROs/FSPs who will handle CTA negotiations, there are a few important questions that can help a sponsor identify the best fit for this crucial study start-up task.

What is the experience of their contract negotiators? How many years negotiating CTAs?

While it is great to have lawyers negotiating contracts of any kind, clinical trial agreement negotiations can certainly be done efficiently with non-attorney staff. The educational degree level is not the most important characteristic of negotiators. Specific and robust CTA negotiation experience should not be ignored. Additionally, although there is sometimes no clear way to identify this in a resume, the people skills of CTA negotiators can make or break any negotiation.

What processes do they have in place for handling negotiations with sites that have an existing sponsor-master CTA?

This is a topic which can cause ample frustration at the sites during CTA negotiations and can easily be avoided. Sponsors must alert the CRO/FSP that master CTAs are in place to avoid having them push the use of a standard CTA agreement for a new study. It is imperative that the CRO/FSP have an established process in place with the sponsor for how to leverage existing master agreements to expedite negotiations from the start.

How will contract negotiator staff turnover be managed during ongoing negotiations?

This topic is rarely proactively discussed between vendor and sponsor, but it is a challenge that happens too often. The sponsor and CRO/FSP should develop a mutually agreed upon plan and proactively communicate knowledge and management of staff turnover during ongoing negotiations.

What is their strategy and plan for getting your CTAs executed quickly?

This question comes loaded with many others: If the negotiations will be handled globally, which countries will be targeted first? Which sites? Will they negotiate directly with all sites or have local affiliates do so? What are the specific country's requirements for CTAs that may have an impact in the agreements being executed quickly? Depending on the answers the CROs/FSPs provide to these questions, the sponsor should be able to gauge their knowledge and experience to get the job done.

What is their CTA negotiation experience within particular countries and regions?

A CRO or FSP may be very experienced in conducting CTA negotiations in the United States and even Europe, but if participating sites are located in South America or the Asia/Pacific region (for example), sponsors need to dig deeper into the CTA negotiation experience of the vendor. The CRO/FSP must be able to appropriately articulate the individual requirements for the selected countries and identify and manage any regulatory or other applicable governing body requirements that may impact the speedy execution of these agreements.

How will site requests for sponsor involvement during negotiations be managed by the CRO/FSP?

No CRO or FSP wants a site communicating directly and solely with the sponsor for CTA negotiations if the vendor is being paid to accomplish this task. However, at times, sites may have legitimate reasons to speak with a contact on the sponsor side. This can happen when negotiations are at a standstill or if the site feels the manner in which negotiations are being handled by the vendor is not appropriate. While no one wants this to happen, it is important that the selected CRO or FSP clearly understands from the start that the investigator and/or site representative should always be provided with a contact at the sponsor if the site desires such information. CROs and FSPs are an extension of the sponsor's brand, and the ease with which they supply contact information during the start-up phase will set the tone for the entire study.

Will a summary of changes approved during negotiations be provided to the sponsor, along with the final CTA version, prior to the full execution of the agreement?

When sponsors hire a CRO or FSP to handle CTA negotiations, time can be lost at finalization if the sponsor does not have a clear understanding of what language or terms were agreed to during negotiations. It is extremely helpful when a summary of approved items is provided to the sponsor prior to final signatures. This way, the sponsor signatory can ensure that the final document only contains items that are within the parameters of the organizations' policies, without needing to hold the document for days to review it line by line.

How will metrics and issues during CTA negotiations be communicated to the sponsor? What will be the frequency and method?

Whether via a weekly call or tracker, communication of negotiation status and issues, on a site-by-site basis, is a must between sponsors and CROs/FSPs negotiating clinical trial agreements. Sponsors can use such calls to discuss any pain points or reoccurring themes, confer and potentially develop clearer negotiation parameters based on CRO feedback, or escalate issues or concerns that may threaten the study start-up process. Issues that are not communicated are rarely resolved and often must be revisited during study conduct.

What is their reputation among sites?

This one is tricky. While everyone one has a bad day, a bad week, or even a bad year, consistently negative feedback from sites on a particular

CRO/FSP or other vendor should be a red flag for sponsors during the vendor-selection process. Feedback can be either formal or informal, but it should be taken under advisement and careful consideration when selecting who will represent you as the sponsor in CTA negotiations for outsourced trials.

What Can Sites Do?

Initiate the Discussion

Who says a site must wait for the sponsor or CRO to initiate CTA negotiations? Once you receive the sponsor or CRO contact information for a study, go ahead and contact them directly via a phone call or email. Being proactive in establishing this first interaction puts you in the forefront of their mind, begins a relationship with the negotiator, and accelerates the conversation.

Outsourced Negotiations Checklist Questions

- Is it appropriate to outsource CTA negotiations for:
    - ○ your organization?
    - ○ specific studies?
    - ○ region(s) of the world?
- What is the experience level of potential CRO/FSP negotiators with CTA negotiations?
- What processes do they have in place for sites with existing sponsor-master clinical trial agreements?
- How will CTA negotiator staff turnover be managed during ongoing negotiations?
- What is their strategy and plan for getting your CTAs executed quickly?
- What is their CTA negotiation experience within specific countries and regions?
- How will site requests to contact the sponsor during negotiations be handled?

- Will a summary of what was approved during negotiations be provided, along with the final CTA version, prior to full execution of the agreement?
- How will metrics and issues during negotiations be communicated to the sponsor? What will be the frequency?
- What is their reputation in the industry and among sites?

CHAPTER 3

Villain #3: Lack of Industry Adoption and Innovation

Villain Name: ADOPTAPHOBIA AND INNOVAPHOBIA SYNDROME

No one can win every battle, but no man should fall without a struggle!
—Spiderman

The next villain is a two-for-one, double-trouble called the adoptaphobia and innovaphobia syndrome. (For the language scholars out there, please don't ping me for not following the Greek language rules—hey, it's catchy!) Despite the focus on innovation at conferences, TED Talks, and other forums in the last few years, as an industry, we are still very slow to innovate and even slower to adopt new technologies, best practices, and methods. In the realm of CTA negotiations, this is no different. Let's first tackle the fear of adoption in our industry—enter *adoptaphobia*.

Adoptaphobia

Despite the focus on innovation at conferences, TED talks, and other forums in the last few years, as an industry we are still very slow to innovate and even slower to adopt new technologies, best practices, and methods. This intense fear of adoption in our industry is what I affectionately call "adoptaphobia." Adoptaphobia refers to our industry's fear of and reluctance to adopting new initiatives, best practices, and technologies to create efficiencies and reduce redundancies. We love to talk about issues and deliberate and discuss new methods, but we are extremely slow to commit and adopt the recommendations and methods that we agree would make everyone's lives easier and streamline the process.

A historical and very familiar example of adoptaphobia within clinical trials can be seen by our industry's slow adoption of electronic data capture (EDC). Despite the advantages that EDC showed early on by reducing double data entry, reducing query rates, and overall streamlining the data collection process for clinical trials, it took well over a decade for the industry in general to fully make the adoption. Today, EDC is the standard method for data collection in clinical trials, as even the thought of conducting a trial using paper collection methods seems wildly archaic and unproductive. Can you imagine trying to move into digital and remote trials today without the adoption of EDC? However, one must wonder how much further along we would be as an industry had we not taken so long to fully embrace this game-changing technology and method. Would we have achieved faster results and gotten needed drugs to market faster? Perhaps. So how does this villain contribute to CTA delays?

Throughout the years, there have been multiple initiatives, discussions, and presentations on the value of adopting industry-wide templates and best practices in the United States and other countries to speed up the negotiation process of CTAs, but it seems that very, very few are adopted.

It seems to be an endless waiting game to see which big players in the industry—both from the sponsor and site side—will make the first move that everyone else can learn from or follow. In the realm of CTA negotiations and other closely associated topics (e.g., site payments), this is no different. I can see two distinct camps in this quandary: those who want an industry-wide standardization of CTA language and templates and those who are skeptical.

The desire of those wanting the standardization is simple. The standardization by all parties in the process will very likely speed up the negotiations and get CTAs executed faster. The reluctance for those who are skeptical likely stems from the averseness to being the only adopters of the new standard or method and that others may not follow suit.

Well, what is the traditional treatment for any phobia? Small, slow, steady exposure to the source of the phobia for desensitization. In this case, it would be small, slow, and steady progress toward the adoption of industry standardization methods and best practices.

How to Defeat This Villain

To speed up CTA execution, we can start by educating ourselves on some of the current industry initiatives that have proven to be helpful and beginning conversations—within both sponsors and sites—on taking "small" steps toward the adoption of these initiatives. I am not suggesting the adoption of every industry trend or initiative merely for the sake of adoption. I am suggesting we begin by taking small steps toward adopting trends or initiatives that work for both the sponsor and site organizations and streamlines current processes.

Adoptaphobia, like any other phobia, is irrational, illogical, and unreasonable in its basic form. Let's explore a few options on how to defeat this villain.

Adopt Master Clinical Trial Agreements

One useful and often underutilized way to speed up CTA negotiations is through the one-time negotiation of a master clinical trial agreement between the sponsor and the investigator site. Skeptics of these types of negotiations usually point to the length of time needed to conclude these negotiations and the disbelief that it saves future negotiation time due to other "villains" that need to be addressed in each new trial (i.e. budget). In other words, the main concern is if the return on investment (ROI) will be a positive one. Sponsors and sites may have limited resources available for negotiations and very lean departments that are already overloaded with negotiating individual CTAs for each study. However, if appropriately timed, master agreement negotiations can be achieved nearly in parallel with a standard CTA negotiation.

Sponsors and sites can utilize the final version of a standard, fully vetted CTA as the starting point for a master clinical trial agreement, eliminating the need to negotiate any of the language that was just approved by both parties. Strategically timing the negotiation of a master agreement upon the conclusion of a standard CTA negotiation capitalizes on the momentum of the sponsor-site relationship and successful negotiation to gain a huge future efficiency in the master agreement negotiations for both parties.

By negotiating master agreements at the conclusion of a standard CTA negotiation, the investment of time from both parties can be significantly less than starting the negotiations from scratch. It is true that other villains such as site budgets may still need to be addressed for each new study. However, since the legal language is currently the main villain threatening the expeditious execution of CTAs, with a master clinical trial agreement in place, you can eliminate this ringleader and decrease the timing of these negotiations by weeks.

Explore Initiatives Such as CLEAR

In my attempt to contribute to the annihilation of our industry's adoptaphobia, I would like to highlight just one of the latest industry initiatives that addresses and streamlines one of the most complex issues in CTA negotiations—the legal language. Enter the CLEAR initiative. The CLEAR (Common Language Evaluation and Reconciliation) initiative was developed through the Society for Clinical Research Sites (SCRS) with the support of TransCelerate BioPharma, Inc. (TransCelerate) and the Association for Clinical Research Organizations (ACRO). It also included stakeholders from various sponsors, sites and CROs. It is important to note that this initiative will continue to evolve as the industry evolves. It is not a model CTA template, but it rather addresses the five key CTA clauses that can add the most negotiation time: indemnification, intellectual property, publication, subject injury, and confidentiality.[8]

Below you will find a quick overview of each, an explanation for why each is so important to both sponsors and sites, and the proposed common language offered by the CLEAR initiative. The proposed language highlighted here is included with the permission of SCRS and comes directly from the CLEAR 2016 white paper developed by Society for

---

[8] "White Papers." Society for Clinical Research Sites SCRS. August 2016. Accessed February 28, 2018. http://myscrs.org/learningcampus/white-papers/

Clinical Research Sites (SCRS). The full white paper can be downloaded for free here: http://myscrs.org/downloads/download-id/6626/.
Indemnification

Why It Is So Important in Simple Terms

This section is used by both the sponsor and site to manage the risk of participating in the clinical trial in the event something goes wrong. The sponsor generally wants to limit when it will "indemnify, defend, and hold harmless" the site, and the site wants this definition to be broader in scope.

Proposed Language from CLEAR Initiative for Industry Adoption

> (a) Sponsor shall indemnify, defend, and hold harmless Institution, the Study Personnel and the Principal Investigator (collectively, the "Indemnitees") from and against any and all liabilities, damages, losses, claims, and expenses, including court costs and reasonable attorneys' fees ("Losses") resulting from or arising out of any third-party claims, actions or proceedings arising out of (i) personal injury to or death of any Study subject enrolled in the Study, which injury or death is caused by (a) the Study Drug used in accordance with the Protocol and this Agreement, or (b) the performance of any procedure required by the Protocol (that would not occur but for the participation in the Study) or Sponsor's written instructions; (ii) Sponsor's use or publication of Study Data; or (iii) Sponsor's and Sponsor's employees', contractors' and agents' negligent acts, omissions or willful misconduct related to the Study or Sponsor's obligations under this Agreement, in each case to the extent that such Losses do not arise out of any Indemnitee's (A) failure to comply with this Agreement, the Protocol, any written instructions of Sponsor concerning the Study, or any Applicable Law, or (B) negligence or willful misconduct. Notwithstanding

the above, medically necessary deviations from the Protocol for reasons of Study Subject safety shall not nullify Sponsor's indemnification obligations, as long as such deviations are consistent with prevailing standards of medical care. (b) Indemnification Procedures. An Indemnitee claiming a right of indemnification or defense under this Agreement shall provide Sponsor with prompt written notice of any such claim(including a copy thereof) served upon it, and shall cooperate fully with Sponsor and its legal representatives in the investigation of any matter regarding the subject of indemnification, at Sponsor's expense; provided, however, that failure by an Indemnitee to provide prompt notice shall not relieve Sponsor of its obligations hereunder except to the extent that Sponsor is prejudiced by such failure. Sponsor shall have the right to exercise sole control over the defense and settlement of any such complaint or claims for which indemnification or defense is sought, including the sole right to select defense counsel and to direct the defense or settlement of any such claim or suit; provided, that Sponsor shall not enter into any non-monetary settlement or admit fault or liability on behalf of any Indemnitee without the prior written consent of such Indemnitee, which consent shall not be unreasonably withheld, conditioned or delayed. An Indemnitee shall have the right to select and to obtain representation by separate legal counsel at the Indemnitee's sole expense. (c) Survival: This Section shall survive termination or expiration of the Agreement.

Publication Rights

Why It Is So Important in Simple Terms

This section is important because it addresses the guidelines for publishing clinical trial results and discusses the timing, breath of information, and methods used for this publication. The sponsor's goal is to ensure protection of the sponsor's intellectual property and confidential information—while still allowing for a site's academic freedom and desire to contribute to the public's knowledge and future research (among other things).[9]

Proposed Language from CLEAR Initiative for Industry Adoption

> (a) Publication and Disclosure. Institution and Principal Investigator shall have the right to publish or present the results of Institution's and Principal Investigator's activities conducted under this Agreement, including Study Data, only in accordance with the requirements of this Section, and provided such publication does not constitute a violation of Section (Confidentiality). Institution and Principal Investigator agree to submit any proposed publication, abstract or presentation, whether in any written, electronic, oral or audio-visual, related to the Study (each, a "Publication") to Sponsor for review at least forty-five (45) days prior to submitting any such proposed Publication to a publisher or proceeding with such proposed presentation. Within forty-five (45) days of such receipt, Sponsor shall advise Institution and/or Principal Investigator, as the case may be, in writing of any information contained therein that is Confidential Information or that may be required for protection of Sponsor's Intellectual Property. Sponsor shall have the right to require Institution and/or Principal Investigator, as applicable, to remove specifically identified Confidential Information and/or to delay the proposed Publication for an additional seventy-five (75) days to

---

[9] Coggin, K. Balancing the Needs of Sponsors and Research Sites to Effectively and Efficiently Negotiate Clinical Trial Agreements. www.butlersnow.com. http://www.butlersnow.com/wp-content/uploads/2016/05/ProTe_Winter-2016_-Balancing-the-Needs-of-Sponsors-and-Research-Sites-to-Effectively-and-Efficiently-Negotiate-Clinical-Trial-Agreements.pdf. (Retrieved October 13, 2017).

enable Sponsor to seek protection of Sponsor's Intellectual Property. (b) Multi-Center Publications. If the Study is a multi-center study, Institution and Principal Investigator agree that they shall not, without the Sponsor's prior written consent, publish, present or otherwise disclose any results of or information pertaining to Institution's and Principal Investigator's activities conducted under this Agreement until a multicenter publication is published; provided, however, that if a multi-center publication is not published within eighteen (18) months after completion of the Study and database lock at all research sites or any earlier termination or abandonment of the Study, Institution and Principal Investigator shall have the right to publish and present the results of Institution's and Principal Investigator's activities conducted under this Agreement, including Study Data, in accordance with the provisions of this Section. (c) For all Publications relating to the Study or including any Study Data, each of Sponsor, Institution and Principal Investigator agrees to comply with all ethical standards concerning publications and authorship as established by the International Committee of Medical Journal Editors ("ICMJE") (found at http://www.icmje.org). (d) Registry and Reporting. Sponsor will register the Study with a public clinical trials registry in accordance with Applicable Law and will report the results of the Study publicly when and to the extent required by Applicable Law. (e) Survival. This Section shall survive termination or expiration of the Agreement.

Intellectual Property

Why It Is So Important in Simple Terms

This section is important because it focuses on ownership of any inventions, discoveries, developments, or improvements related to the clinical trial or investigational drug (or both). Sponsors generally desire broader language in the ownership of all inventions and discoveries, while sites want to limit this ownership to allow for instances where the site may pioneer an invention of its own.[10]

Proposed Language from CLEAR Initiative for Industry Adoption

> (a) Pre-existing Intellectual Property. Ownership of inventions, discoveries, works of authorship, processes, procedures and other developments existing as of the Effective Date, and all patents, copyrights, trade secret rights and other intellectual property rights therein (collectively, "Pre-existing Intellectual Property"), is not affected by this Agreement, and no party shall have any claims to or rights in any Pre-existing Intellectual Property of the other party, except as may be otherwise expressly provided in a separate written agreement between the parties. (b) All Intellectual Property arising from and relating to the Study, the Study Drug (including but not limited to its formulation and use alone or in combination with other drugs) or the Protocol (collectively "Sponsor Intellectual Property") shall vest exclusively in the Sponsor. For clarity, Sponsor Intellectual Property excludes any clinical procedures or other processes or procedures relating in general to the conduct of clinical trials and improvements thereto that are the procedures of the Institution. (c) Disclosure and Assignment. Principal Investigator and Institution shall, and shall ensure that their Study Personnel, disclose all Sponsor Intellectual Property promptly and fully to Sponsor in writing, and Principal Investigator and

---

[10] Coggin, K. Balancing the Needs of Sponsors and Research Sites to Effectively and Efficiently Negotiate Clinical Trial Agreements. www.butlersnow.com. http://www.butlersnow.com/wp-content/uploads/2016/05/ProTe_Winter-2016_-Balancing-the-Needs-of-Sponsors-and-Research-Sites-to-Effectively-and-Efficiently-Negotiate-Clinical-Trial-Agreements.pdf. (Retrieved October 13, 2017).

Institution hereby assign, and shall ensure that their Study Personnel assign to Sponsor all of its rights, title and interest in and to all Sponsor Intellectual Property, including all patents, copyrights and other intellectual property rights contained therein, (but excluding patient medical records), and all rights of action and claims for damages and benefits arising due to past and present infringement of said rights.

The Principal Investigator and Institution shall cooperate and assist Sponsor, at Sponsor's expense, by executing and ensuring that their Study Personnel execute, all documents reasonably necessary for Sponsor to secure and maintain Sponsor's ownership rights in the Sponsor Intellectual Property. (d) License. Sponsor hereby grants to Institution a perpetual, non-exclusive, non-transferable, paid-up license, without right to sublicense, to use the Study Data, subject to the obligations set forth in Section (Confidentiality), for its own internal research and educational purposes (all of which must be non-commercial purposes), and for publications, presentations and public disclosures in accordance with Section (Publication Rights). (e) Patent Prosecution. Institution and Principal Investigator shall reasonably cooperate, at Sponsor's request and expense, with Sponsor's preparation, filing, prosecution, and maintenance of all patent applications and patents for Sponsor Intellectual Property. (f) Survival. This Section shall survive termination or expiration of this Agreement.

Confidentiality

Why It Is So Important in Simple Terms

This section addresses what information within or arising out of the clinical trial will be considered confidential and the obligations of both sponsor and site to maintain this confidentiality. One of the main areas of tension in this section lies in the sponsor's desire to maintain confidentiality of any information generated or provided throughout the trial and the site's desire to maintain the academic freedom to share information for reasons such as public welfare and to promote further research.[11]

Proposed Language from CLEAR Initiative for Industry Adoption

(a) Definition. "Confidential Information" means the confidential and proprietary information of Sponsor and includes without limitation: (i) all information disclosed by or on behalf of Sponsor to Institution, Principal Investigator or Study Personnel, including without limitation, the Study Drug, technical information relating to the Study Drug, all Preexisting Intellectual Property of Sponsor, Sponsor's Intellectual Property and the Protocol; and (ii) Study enrollment information, information pertaining to the status of the Study, communications to and from regulatory authorities, information relating to the regulatory status of the Study Drug, and Study Data. Confidential Information shall not include information that: (i) can be shown by documentation to have been public knowledge prior to or after disclosure by Sponsor, other than through wrongful acts or omissions attributable to Principal Investigator, Institution or Study Personnel; (ii) can be shown by documentation to have been in the possession of Principal Investigator, Institution or Study Personnel prior to disclosure by Sponsor, from sources other than Sponsor without restriction as to use or confidentiality; or (iii) can be shown by documentation to have been independently developed by Principal Investigator, Institution or Study Personnel. (b) Obligations. Institution, Principal Investigator and Study Personnel shall not: (i) use

---

[11] Leibowitz, K., & Sheckler, V. Negotiating Clinical Trial Agreements. www.hoganlovells.ru. http://www.hoganlovells.ru/files/Publication/feb6c0eb-127a-4064-882a-926352a2baea/Presentation/PublicationAttachment/e474b2c6-bb90-489d-9de5-e721c2ee1c8a/Leibowitz%20Sheckler%20article.pdf. Retrieved October 13, 2017

Confidential Information for any purpose other than the performance of the Study, aggregate and de-identified (as to Sponsor or Study) metric reporting to third parties and for internal training and quality assurance purposes; or (ii) disclose Confidential Information to any third party, except as permitted by this Section and by Section (Publication Rights), or as may be required by law or by a regulatory authority or as authorized in writing by the disclosing party. To protect Confidential Information, Institution and the Principal Investigator agree to: (i) limit dissemination of Confidential Information to only those personnel having a "need to know"; (ii) advise all personnel who receive Confidential Information of the confidential nature of such information; and (iii) protect Confidential Information from disclosure. Nothing herein shall limit the right of Institution and Principal Investigator to disclose Study Data as permitted by Section (Publication Rights) or as may be required during the informed consent process. (c) Compelled Disclosure. In the event that Institution or Principal Investigator receives notice from a third party seeking to compel disclosure of any Confidential Information, the notice recipient shall provide Sponsor with notice as promptly as possible so that Sponsor may seek a protective order or other appropriate remedy, unless prohibited by Applicable Law. In the event that such protective order or other remedy is not obtained, the notice recipient shall furnish only that portion of the Confidential Information which is legally required to be disclosed, and shall request confidential treatment for such Confidential Information. (d) Return or Destruction. Upon termination of this Agreement or upon any earlier written request by Sponsor at any time, Institution and Principal Investigator shall return to Sponsor, or destroy, at Sponsor's option and expense, all Confidential Information other than as may be permitted by Section (Publication Rights), except that Institution and the Principal Investigator may retain one copy of such Confidential Information in a secure location for archival purposes and ongoing compliance under the Agreement, and thereafter make no use of the Confidential Information whatsoever. Any Confidential Information retained in computer backups shall be maintained in accordance with this Agreement. (e) Survival. This Section shall survive termination or expiration of this Agreement for seven (7) Years.

Study Subject Injury

Why It Is So Important in Simple Terms

This section describes the type of reimbursement the sponsor will provide to the clinical trial participant in the event of a trial-related injury. Whether or not the sponsor will reimburse medical expenses for any trial participant's injuries is usually the biggest point of dispute. The main areas of disagreement between sponsor and site are how and by whom causation and determination of the injury will be made, how preexisting injuries will be treated, what monetary value will be offered to address injury treatment, and whether reimbursement will first need to be sought from private insurers by the site.[12]

Proposed Language from CLEAR Initiative for Industry Adoption

If a Study Subject suffers an adverse reaction, illness, or injury that was caused by the Study Drug or any procedure performed in accordance with the Protocol (one that would not have been performed but for their participation in the Study), or as the result of any actions taken at the written instruction of Sponsor,

---

[12] Coggin, K. Balancing the Needs of Sponsors and Research Sites to Effectively and Efficiently Negotiate Clinical Trial Agreements. www.butlersnow.com. http://www.butlersnow.com/wp-content/uploads/2016/05/ProTe_Winter-2016_-Balancing-the-Needs-of-Sponsors-and-Research-Sites-to-Effectively-and-Efficiently-Negotiate-Clinical-Trial-Agreements.pdf. (Retrieved October 13, 2017).

Sponsor shall pay for the reasonable and necessary costs of medical diagnosis and treatment of such injuries. Notwithstanding the foregoing, Sponsor shall not be liable for expenses that are arise as a result of (i) negligence or willful misconduct on the party of the Principal Investigator, Institution or Study Personnel, or (ii) the natural progression of an underlying or pre-existing condition or events, unless exacerbated by participation in the Study.

What Can Sites Do?

Join the Discussion

Don't wait for sponsors to initiate the conversation about negotiating a master clinical trial agreement or other industry initiatives such as CLEAR. Upon the conclusion of a standard CTA negotiation (or even during), ask about negotiating a master CTA. These agreements are helpful to the sponsor, will streamline the process for investigator sites, and will make future interactions on the subject inherently easier.

Innovaphobia

Innovaphobia, in many ways, can be even more dangerous. Despite clinical trial agreement delays being a pain point for many years, the industry has been extremely slow to innovate in this specific area in terms of technologies, processes, and shifts in the paradigm of CTA negotiations. Though we have seen many new technologies and platforms in the past few years that can also be used to assist in CTA negotiations, very few have been built with CTA negotiations in mind from the beginning.

To effectively address CTA negotiation delays now and, in the future, we must not solely rely on the current tools and processes. We *must* innovate in this field. The sections that follow contain a few conversation and idea starters (and even potential business opportunities) for how we can bring innovation to this specific area of our industry and defeat this villain. This is in no way an exhaustive list. It is simply designed to spark much needed conversations and action.

Débora S. Araujo

How to Defeat This Villain

Idea: FMV Industry Alignment

FMV within clinical trials is an area addressed by federal guidelines, but it still contains a whole lot of blurriness. For both sponsors and sites, maintaining fair and impartial market values while negotiating the budget can require a great deal of effort. Both the sponsor and the site typically create their own FMV process and attempt to adhere to it, while still trying to negotiate an apples-to-oranges budget scenario. Aligning as an industry on basic FMV parameters or developing a FMV mathematical formula could create consistency and introduce efficiencies. Potentially, this approach could decrease or even eliminate the need for negotiation of budgets created within and abiding by industry-wide FMV parameters. Imagine the day we are all speaking the same language in the world of site budget negotiations? It can happen but we must come to the table and align as an industry on this topic.

Idea: Central FMV-Determining Body

Major FMV efficiencies can also be created in CTA negotiations if a central FMV-determining organization is used—similar to the current use of central IRBs. Similar initiatives have been recently launched in other countries such as Canada in the attempt to streamline and standardize this very complex process. The central FMV-determining body can be an independent entity that lacks any connection to the sponsor, the site, or the clinical trial in question. Once site budgets are approved by this independent organization, all parties can be comfortable knowing all due diligence has been done in conformity with acceptable industry standards. This could eliminate the need for sponsors and sites to create their own individual FMV processes, while bringing ease and protection to both parties. Sites can be certain that their costs for performing the clinical trial are covered, and sponsors can feel comfortable approving costs requested by sites with greater ease without the fear of the perception of impropriety.

Idea: Technology to Expedite CTA negotiations

This one is one of my favorites. Here we are in an age where virtual reality is easily accessible, we are diving into conducting fully remote and digital clinical trials, we have things ordered by Alexa™ yet much of our CTA negotiations are done semi-manually in Microsoft Word and via e-mail. While these traditional tools still serve a purpose, we need to leverage the technology advances we must disrupt the way we currently work. The technology to expedite CTA negotiations needs to go beyond a repository or a portal for document exchange. It needs to use our advancements in technology to cut down on negotiation time and assist negotiators by providing language and other suggestions that meet both parties' negotiation parameters—while not putting either party at legal or financial risk. There is a need for technology innovations in this area that can leverage previously negotiated items and language to jump-start CTA negotiations and close the deal. By exploring all that is at our disposal in this digital era, we can catapult our advancement in the negotiations of these agreements in minimal time.

Industry Adoption and Innovation Checklist

Industry Adoption

- explore negotiating (and using) master clinical trial agreements
- explore the adoption of industry initiatives such as CLEAR to streamline your CTA negotiation process. Full whitepaper can be downloaded for free here: http://myscrs.org/downloads/download-id/6626/
    - indemnification
    - publication rights
    - intellectual property
    - confidentiality
    - study subject injury

Débora S. Araujo

Industry Innovation

- FMV industry alignment
- central FMV-determining body
- technology to expedite CTA negotiations

CHAPTER 4

Villain #4: All the Other Things Affecting CTA Negotiations

Villain Name: MR. PERIPHERAL

> You're going to make a difference. A lot of times it won't be huge,
> it won't be visible even. But it will matter just the same.
> —Commissioner James Gordon (*Batman*)

There is sentiment in our industry that if there is no more tea in China, you can blame it on contract delays. Clinical contract and/or budget negotiations are very often blamed for the majority of study start-up delays. While there is an element of truth in this (thus the reason for this book), there is also a great deal of generalization, which is true of most sayings. Let me provide a real-world example.

A while back, I attended an industry conference at which one of the attendees mentioned that her organization (a large sponsor) had taken many of the steps outlined in this book and had successfully slashed their average CTA negotiation cycle in half. Her accomplishment was quickly met with cynicism when the start-up period of a new study was significantly delayed due to the classic CTA bottleneck. However, upon further investigation, it was discovered that the CTA negotiations were at a standstill—not because of the usual legal language and site-budget discussions—but because the site had never received the study lab manual!

The site required this document to do their internal coverage analysis and budget preparation in order to continue negotiations.

This is a perfect example of our next villain: Mr. Peripheral. The reality is that, sometimes, we are so focused on the actual task of negotiating a CTA that we miss the supporting and peripheral tasks that go along with it. It is vital that we take a closer look within our organizations to make sure that all the peripheral, supportive functions and processes needed for CTA negotiations are known, aligned, and providing the expected contributions. This is a concept that can be applied to both sponsor and investigator sites. Let's explore a few options on how to defeat this villain.

How to Defeat This Villain

Be Aware and Leverage Other Study Start-Up Activities

Confidentiality Disclosure Agreements (CDAs)

Before any substantial conversations about a specific clinical trial can begin, sponsors need to collect signed CDAs from any sites that desire to participate in the study. The process can delay study start-up if sites want to negotiate the language in these agreements or if multiple CDAs are required by the site for principal investigator, sub-investigator, and institution, for example.[13]

Prestudy Visit

The prestudy visit takes place at some point after a CDA has been executed and the site feasibility questionnaire (SFQ) has been answered by the site. This is an opportunity for the sponsor and the site to get to know more about each other and discuss the site's ability to perform the clinical trial effectively.

The important thing about these prestudy visits as they relate to CTA negotiations is that sponsors and CROs/FSPs often wait until after these

---

[13] Chung, J. "10 Steps to Clinical Study Startup." Www.goBalto.com. Accessed November 27, 2017. https://www.gobalto.com/blog/2010/05/12/10-steps-to-clinical-study-startup-step-3-sending-cdas-to-sites/

visits to send the proposed budget and CTA template to sites. However, if the budget and CTA are sent prior to the prestudy visits, sites have more time to review them prior to preparing for regulatory submissions.[13] As well, early provision of the budget and CTA allows for early detection of CTA language and budget problems. Both parties will know whether or not agreement can be reached earlier—before investing too much time in the process.

Regulatory Document Submissions

Prior to enrolling subjects in a clinical trial, there are regulatory submissions that must happen both at the federal agency and IRB/EC level. It is especially important for sponsors and CROs/FSPs to clearly understand and track the unique regulatory requirements for each individual investigator site. Some sites will not be ready to prepare regulatory documents until the clinical trial agreement and accompanying budget have been fully negotiated. In such cases, sending the CTA documents after a CDA is in place but prior to the prestudy visit can give the site sufficient time to review and negotiate the documents and avoid delaying regulatory submissions. [13]

Local versus Central IRB Sites

In the United States, a site can choose to use either a central or local institutional review board (IRB) for multicenter clinical trials. Investigator sites using a local IRB have historically required more time to gain approval, adding to the study start-up timelines. However, in the past few years, there has been a global push for the centralization of IRBs and ethics committees.[14]

In June 2017, the NIH finalized its policy on using a single IRB (sIRB) for NIH-funded multisite studies. This policy reinforces the recommendation by other federal agencies for a centralized review by a central IRB for multisite clinical research. This has also created more pressure for all parties involved in clinical research in general to explore the more frequent use of central IRBs versus local IRBs. This is a trend that may impact overall study start-up in the next few years.[15]

Regulatory Requirements—Country and Site

Take the time to understand if the countries and sites on your list have specific requirements, such as regularly used model agreements, unique regulatory requirements and timelines affecting the CTA execution, special approval requirements other than regulatory bodies, parties that need to be involved in negotiations, and any other unique situations.

Many of the issues that result in delays in CTA execution can be solved by proactively seeking business intelligence. A firm understanding of the needs of specific countries and sites being used for a study is of vital importance—and so is appropriately planning and preparing for them. For example, some sites may have various internal committees that need to review the study documents before CTA negotiations can begin. Obtaining this information prior to the start of negotiations is extremely helpful in minimizing frustration in the process. This approach

---

[14] Schimanski, Carolann. "Streamline and Improve Study Start-Up." Applied Clinical Trials Home. October 16, 2017. Accessed October 21, 2017. http://www.appliedclinicaltrialsonline.com/streamline-and-improve-study-start.

[15] Pyle, S. "Benefits of Centralized IRB Review." SCHULMAN IRB. May 25, 2017. Accessed October 27, 2017. http://www.sairb.com/benefits-of-centralized-irb-review/

is important whether a sponsor is conducting a study in its home country or in multiple countries.

Unique Country Requirements for CTAs

For those working with CTA negotiations only in the United States, the peripherals will be mostly related to individual site requirements and timelines. However, when thinking about CTA negotiations outside of the United States, additional country requirements must be considered when planning study start-up. These requirements may be country-specific model agreements and budget templates, sponsor obligations, ethics and regulatory approvals, insurance requirements, or others. It is important to obtain this intelligence on the specific country requirements early and to utilize those with the greatest level of expertise for CTA negotiations in those countries.

Following are a few unique requirements for specific countries that may be helpful to keep in mind. (A more extensive list of unique country requirements is included at the end of this book for reference.)

Spain

Spain has seventeen regions, and each region has its own agreement template. Sites will usually want to have the sponsor's insurance information before the CTA can be finalized. When working with public hospitals, the site's contract template is most frequently used, and there is a requirement that the sponsor listed in the contract be established in the European Union (EU).[16]

India

As delineated in the IN-GCPs, before the trial begins, the sponsor or the CRO must sign a formal legal agreement or contract with each participating institution. If no institutions are involved, the individual investigator's

---

[16] Buckley, Helene. "Dispelling Myths – Site Contracting in Italy, Spain and UK". https://www.linkedin.com/pulse/dispelling-myths-site-contracting-italy-spain-uk-helene-buckley/. (Retrieved on October 27, 2017).

signature is required. The contract should define the relationship between the sponsor and the investigator/institution in terms of financial support, fees, honorarium, and payments in kind. The sponsor or the CRO must also agree to

- conduct the trial in compliance with the IN-GCPs, the applicable regulatory requirements, and the clinical trial protocol agreed to by the sponsor and approved by the EC;
- comply with the procedures for data recording and reporting;
- retain the trial-related essential documents until he or she informs the investigator(s)/institution(s) in writing that these documents are no longer needed; and
- permit clinical trial-site inspections by DCGI authorized officers, as per the IN-GCPs and the DCR-2ndAmdmt.[17]

For more information on the requirements for conducting a clinical trial in India along with CTA requirements, go to https://clinregs.niaid.nih.gov/single_country.php?c_id=30#trial_initiation.

Italy

Sites will not sign clinical trial agreements until they have received approval from the local ethics committee (LEC). The contract templates used are those of the site and are generally required to be in the local language. An EU sponsor is also required in the agreement.[16]

United Kingdom

Public hospitals will utilize the ABPI template and sponsors should use the UK budget template tool for those negotiations. An EU sponsor is required on the agreement.[16]

---

[17] National Institute of Allergy and Infectious Diseases. Accessed November 27, 2017. https://clinregs.niaid.nih.gov/single_country.php?c_id=199

France

For public hospitals, the site budget must be agreed upon with the national coordinator before it is discussed with the other study sites in France. The country CTA template and budget tool should be used. An EU sponsor is required on the agreement.[18]

South Africa

According to the SA-GCPs, before the trial begins, a sponsor must prepare a written agreement that includes any information not covered in the protocol. The agreement must be signed by the sponsor, the PI, and any other parties involved with the trial to confirm the contract terms.[19] The sponsor should also obtain the investigator's agreement to

- conduct the trial in compliance with the SA-GCPs, the MCC requirements, and with the EC approved protocol;
- comply with data recording/reporting procedures;
- permit monitoring, auditing, and inspection; and
- retain the trial-related essential documents until the sponsor informs the investigator(s) and institution(s) that these documents are no longer needed.

The financial considerations of the trial should also be documented in the agreement. A declaration must be signed by the sponsor and PI stating that sufficient funds are available to complete the clinical study.[19]

For more information on the requirements for conducting a clinical trial in South Africa along with CTA requirements, go to https://clinregs.niaid.nih.gov/single_country.php?c_id=30#trial_initiation.

---

[18] Buckley, Helene. "Same Story Different Day CTA SIV". https://www.linkedin.com/pulse/same-story-different-day-cta-siv-helene-buckley/. (Retrieved on November 27, 2017)

[19] National Institute of Allergy and Infectious Diseases. Accessed November 27, 2017. https://clinregs.niaid.nih.gov/single_country.php?c_id=199

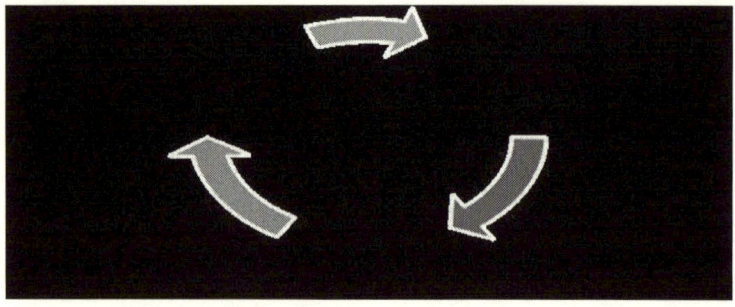

Cumbersome Internal Processes

"The devil is in the details" is a good description for how significant delays can be hidden in something as plain as internal sponsor/CRO processes for CTA negotiations and execution. One thing that can be done (especially from a sponsor perspective) to help address this issue is a thorough review of sponsor/CRO processes for value, efficiency, rationale for use, and customer/patient centricity. What is the value that the process brings to the overall big picture? Is it truly needed or only nice to have? Can we do it better and faster in any other way? Is it customer/patient-centric? Why was it put in place? Is the reason it was put in place still relevant? By asking these questions, many outdated and redundant internal processes can be identified, corrected, or eliminated.

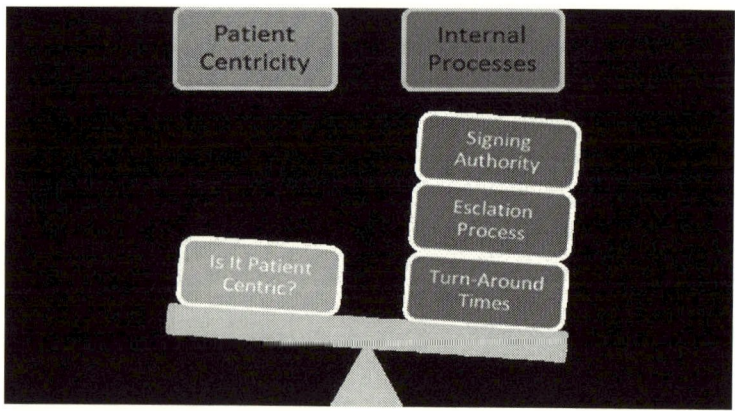

Limited Negotiation Parameters

Sponsors usually have either internal staff negotiating CTAs or have a CRO/vendor handling this task. For midsize and large sponsors (and many sites), the contract negotiators do not typically reside within the legal department and are not necessarily attorneys. Negotiation parameters or a CTA "playbook" is usually developed by the sponsor's (and many sites) legal team and provided to the contract negotiators to aid in the negotiations. Such playbooks are vital to expediting the negotiation process and reducing the need for escalation of routinely requested modifications that the sponsor or site would agree to under certain circumstances.

It is important for sponsors and sites to update their playbooks periodically to reflect routinely requested items or new industry trends for both CTA language and budget. A playbook that is in place but has not been reviewed or updated for three years cannot be very effective since it likely does not reflect current industry trends, requests, or changes. Failing to maintain the playbook and/or neglecting to keep the parameters current and comprehensive defeats the document's purpose of speeding up the negotiation process. The task of periodically reviewing and updating these playbooks will increase the effectiveness of such documents and decrease the need for and cost of escalation to legal departments or outside counsel.

Example of Escalation Layers in CTA Negotiations

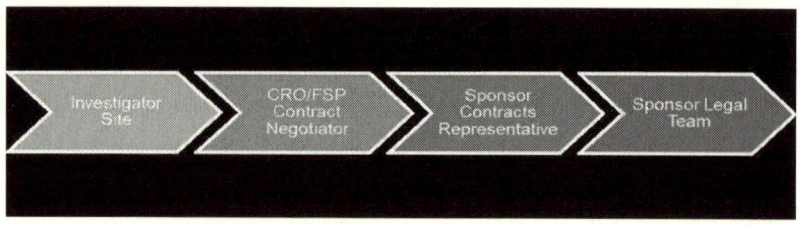

Review Escalation Processes

Both sponsors and sites have escalation processes in place for when requests during negotiations fall into gray areas. These processes are needed to ensure both the sponsor and site are legally protected, especially when the request is unusual in nature. However, such requests can add to the number of days in the negotiation process since they often must go to the legal team of the organization that may be servicing multiple departments and carrying a heavy workload. This obviously translates into a delay in the entire process.

It can be beneficial for escalation processes, like all processes, to be reviewed carefully for redundancy and efficiency. For example, does every one of these requests need to go to a legal team? Can some business decisions versus legal decisions be handled by others in the organization and result in a faster turnaround time? These are only two of the questions that can be asked to identify potential areas where improvement may be warranted.

Staff Workload Issues

At first glance, this topic should be a no-brainer, but staff workload is a big enough problem that it deserves some discussion. Until CTA negotiations can be fully performed by technology or a robot (there's a business idea for someone), real human beings who must eat and sleep will be handling these. This means there is only so much work that can efficiently be done by these negotiators in a day. Many organizations in our industry continue to put the pressure of study start-up on clinical contract negotiations without appropriately resourcing the function or providing the appropriate tools, funds, or flexibility to try doing it in a better way. Appropriately resourcing this function whether at the sponsor, CRO/vendor, or site will help to move CTA negotiations along.

What Can Sites Do?

Let sponsors and CROs/vendors know before starting the negotiation process that there are mandatory internal committee reviews or other requirements that will need to take place before negotiations can begin or proceed. By setting the expectations early on, sites can avoid follow-up emails and phone calls but still assure the sponsor/CRO that negotiations have not been forgotten.

The Peripheral's Checklist

- Confirm other study start-up activities surrounding CTA negotiations and execution are appropriately aligned.
- Confirm specific country and site regulatory/ethics requirements connected to CTA negotiations and execution.
- Set appropriate CTA expectations for local versus central IRB sites for CTA negotiation timelines.
- Confirm individual country guidelines for model agreements, templates, and best practices for CTA negotiations.
- Confirm that internal processes are not getting in the way of negotiations.
- Ensure internal negotiation parameters and playbooks are robust, regularly updated, and reflect current industry practices.

The Peripheral's Questions

- What is the value that the process brings to the overall big picture?
- Is it truly needed or only nice to have?
- Can we do it better and faster in any other way?
- Is it customer/patient-centric?
- Why was it put in place?
- Is the reason it was put in place still relevant?

CHAPTER 5

CTA Delays Symptom Checker

Have you ever visited WebMD.com? They have a tool called a "Symptom Checker" that helps you identify what type of illness you may have based on the symptoms you indicate. You are first asked to answer a series of questions about what you are feeling, and the tool provides you with a list of possible conditions as well as potential treatments. The only caveat is that the broader you are in describing your symptoms, the longer the list of possible (and sometimes outrageous) conditions. The more specific you are about your symptoms, the greater the possibility of the tool giving you a more accurate list of possible conditions and treatments.

Using that same line of thinking, I have listed in the next few pages some classic symptoms of CTA delays, some possible "conditions" that may be causing them, and potential "treatments." As with the WebMD tool, this is meant to be informational, but it is in no way a substitute for a targeted and professional evaluation of your organization, processes, and teams. However, it is a great conversation starter to identify potential causes contributing to CTA negotiation delays.

Symptom

- My organization's overall CTA turnaround times are too long.

Possible Conditions

- lack of efficient oversight-type role for entire process
- staff workload issues
- lack of site/country intelligence and expertise by negotiators
- limited negotiation parameters provided to negotiators
- escalation process not optimal
- a whole lot of other things

Potential Treatments

Establish an oversight-type role to manage the entire CTA negotiation process from the tactical pieces of the actual negotiation and how other areas of the study start-up process may contribute to overall CTA delays.

Review realistically any staff workload issues and address them appropriately. This one is not complicated, but it is very often overlooked.

Ensure that whoever will be handling CTA negotiations has technical expertise as well as expertise for that specific region and/or country. It does not matter if they are in-house staff or outsourced. What matters is that they are experts of their trade and region, truly fit for purpose.

Ensure that contract negotiators have the appropriate tools in place to properly execute their tasks. This includes providing robust and appropriate negotiation parameters and ensuring that any escalation processes are not redundant and inefficient.

The reality is that when someone says that the overall CTA turnaround times for his or her organization are too long, it is like typing *headache* in the WebMD symptom-checker tool. The possible conditions may be many. It is important to drill down and get as specific as you can to properly identify the causes of your CTA delays and effectively deal with them.

Symptom

- While we can get through the language piece of our CTA negotiations quickly, our site-budget negotiations continue to be bottlenecked.

Possible Conditions

- site budgets are not being developed with appropriate FMV parameters
- lack of visibility on procedure-level costs
- sponsor's budget proposal does not include all procedures and costs to conduct the clinical trial at the site
- sponsor's budget proposal has not properly taken into consideration staff time required per visit
- institutional requirements (e.g., use of specifically assigned clinical trial room) at the site necessitates additional funds

Potential Treatments

Ensure that a robust FMV process is put in place to address the different regional and institution variations within a country.

Please do not provide per-visit or per-patient level budgets to sites. These just add to the negotiation time since some sites may be confused about what exactly has been included. Be proactive and provide procedure-level budgets (in a similar structure to the "schedule of events" from the protocol) to potential sites. This transparency will establish a great start to the sponsor/site relationship and move budget negotiations along.

It may seem obvious, but it is important to ensure that all protocol-related procedures and associated costs are covered and listed in the initial budget sent to sites. This very simple point can have a ripple effect across many sites, and needing to correct the mistake after the fact will be an annoyance to all parties involved.

Symptom

- Our CTA negotiations seem to always be the limiting factor that hold things up at the very end of our study start-up process.

Possible Conditions

- sending CTA documents too late in the study start-up process
- unnecessary and cumbersome CTA language and too narrow negotiation parameters
- cumbersome internal processes

Potential Treatments

You may be sending CTA documents too late in the study start-up timeline. Experiment with sending these documents shortly after there is a CDA in place and a SFQ has been received from the site. As soon as there is an interest from both sides to move toward a prestudy visit, CTA documents should be sent to the site to allow for ample review and negotiation time.

Explore if CTA language needs to be streamlined or negotiation parameters broadened to allow for easier execution of these agreements.

Take time to thoroughly review your internal processes for CTA negotiations, escalations, and approvals to identify potential gaps or redundancies that may be causing the bottleneck.

Symptom

- My CRO/FSP is taking longer than expected to negotiate our clinical trial agreements.

Possible Conditions

- lack of CTA negotiation expertise or knowledge of country requirements
- CRO/FSP not leveraging existing master clinical trial agreements

- limited negotiation parameters for CRO/FSP

Potential Treatments

Clarify early in the CRO/FSP engagement how existing master clinical trial agreements will be leveraged in negotiations to speed up the negotiation process and avoid frustration with sites.

Make sure that the negotiation parameters you provide to your CRO/FSP are robust and appropriate in order to decrease the need for unnecessary escalations, pushbacks, and overall negotiation timelines.

Depending on what is causing your CRO/FSP to delay in CTA negotiations, the best thing you can do for your study may be to switch to a better one. This should be your last resort. If there is no way to turn the tide by providing additional training or clearer guidelines and parameters, explore selecting an expert provider for CTA negotiations. This is not the time to get a jack-of-all-trades.

IN CLOSING

Getting Back to Why

The Unintended Consequences of CTA Delays

The impact of delays in CTA execution has gained new meaning in the clinical trial community through the story of T. J. Sharpe. Diagnosed with Stage IV melanoma at age thirty-seven, he found a glimpse of hope in a clinical trial—only to have that hope threatened by a six-week delay in joining the trial due to a CTA not being executed.[20] His story, and countless other examples throughout the years, have prompted industry-wide initiatives that attempt to solve the issue. However, we must have an intimate look at each of the different villains that contribute to clinical trial agreement delays and be willing to address them simultaneously to truly accelerate this process. By addressing this industry issue comprehensively, we can decrease delays in CTA execution, speed up study start-up by weeks, and let patients like T. J. know that we have not only heard them, but that we are listening.

In the words of a lesser known superhero, "Do you want to know who you are? Don't ask. Act! Action will delineate and define you." – Thomas Jefferson.

---

[20] "White Papers." Society for Clinical Research Sites SCRS. August 2016. Accessed February 28, 2018. http://myscrs.org/learningcampus/white-papers/

APPENDIX A

Streamlining CTA Negotiations Checklist

Site-Budget Negotiations

- Provide procedure-level budgets to investigator sites (sponsor).
- Provide CTA documents, including site budgets, early in the study start-up process.
- Tailor site budgets within formal fair market value (FMV) process (sponsor).
- Have and use a fair market value (FMV) process that is (sponsor and site)
    - ○ formal,
    - ○ well documented,
    - ○ consistently applied,
    - ○ reasonable,
    - ○ defensible,
    - ○ passes the ethical test, and
    - ○ has a methodical and logical market data value source
- Have and use a fair market value (FMV) deviation process that is (sponsor and site)
    - ○ formal,
    - ○ well documented,
    - ○ consistently applied for exceptions,
    - ○ reasonable,
    - ○ defensible, and

- ○ passes the ethical test.
- Explore if master-budget negotiations are appropriate (sponsor and site).
- Explore using recently approved fees as start point of negotiations (sponsor).
- Provide justification documents up front in negotiation process (site).

Outsourced Negotiations

Questions for Sponsors to Consider

- Is it appropriate to outsource CTA negotiations for:
    - ○ your organization?
    - ○ which studies?
    - ○ region of the world?
- What is the experience level of their negotiators with CTA negotiations?
- What processes do they have in place for sites with existing sponsor-master clinical trial agreements?
- How will CTA negotiator staff turnover be managed during ongoing negotiations?
- What is their strategy and plan for getting your CTAs executed quickly?
- What is their CTA negotiation experience within specific countries and regions?
- How will site requests to contact the sponsor during negotiations be handled?
- Will a summary of what was approved during negotiations be provided along with the final CTA version prior to full execution of the agreement?
- Will both the executed PDF document as well as the final Word version be provided the sponsor? (Getting the Word version allows for previously negotiated terms to more easily be reused in future CTAs.)
- How will metrics and issues during negotiations be communicated to the sponsor? What will be the frequency?

- What is their reputation in the industry and among sites?

Industry Adoption

- explore negotiating (and using) master clinical trial agreements
- explore the adoption of industry initiatives such as CLEAR to streamline your CTA negotiation process. Full whitepaper can be downloaded for free here: http://myscrs.org/downloads/download-id/6626/
    - indemnification
    - publication rights
    - intellectual property
    - confidentiality
    - study subject injury

Industry Innovation

- Explore the idea of FMV industry alignment.
- Explore the idea of central FMV-determining body.
- Explore the idea of technology to expedite CTA negotiations.

All Other Things Affecting CTA Negotiations—Peripherals

- Confirm other study start-up activities surrounding CTA negotiations and execution are appropriately aligned.
- Confirm specific country and site regulatory/ethics requirements connected to CTA negotiations and execution.
- Set appropriate CTA expectations for local versus central IRB sites for CTA negotiation timelines.
- Confirm the individual country's unique guidelines for model agreements, templates, and best practices for CTA negotiations.
- Confirm that your internal processes are not getting in the way of negotiations.
- Ensure internal negotiation parameters and playbooks are robust, regularly updated, and reflective of current industry practices.

Questions for Sponsors to Consider - Peripherals

- What is the value that the process brings to the overall big picture?
- Is it truly needed or only nice to have?
- Can we do it better and faster in any other way?
- Is it customer/patient-centric?
- Why was it put in place?
- Is the reason it was put in place still relevant?

APPENDIX B

CLEAR™ (Common Language Evaluation and Reconciliation)

Full white paper can be downloaded for free here: http://myscrs.org/downloads/download-id/6626/.

CLEAR™ Definitions[21]

"Agreement" means this agreement comprising its clauses, schedules, and any appendices attached to it.

"Applicable Law" means all of the statutes, regulations, rules, and guidelines, including without limitation, Regulatory Authority rules and guidelines relating to the conduct of the Clinical Trial, ICH GCP, and federal and state (replace with "provincial" in Canada) privacy legislation and data protection laws that apply to the conduct of the Clinical Trial by the Institution, the Principal Investigator and Sponsor.

"Intellectual Property" means patents, trademarks, trade names, trade secrets, service marks, domain name copyrights, moral rights, rights in and to databases (including rights to prevent the extraction or reutilization of information from a database), design rights, topography rights and all rights or forms of protection of a similar nature or having equivalent or the similar effect to any of them which may subsist anywhere in the world, whether or not any of

---

[21] "White Papers." Society for Clinical Research Sites SCRS. August 2016. Accessed February 28, 2018. http://myscrs.org/learningcampus/white-papers/

them are registered and including applications for registration of any of them. Intellectual Property includes all and any technical and other information which is not in the public domain (other than as a result of a breach of confidence), including but not limited to information comprising or relating to concepts, discoveries, data, designs, formulae, ideas, inventions, methods, models, procedures, materials, substances, designs for experiments and tests and results of experimentation and testing, processes, specifications and techniques, laboratory records, clinical data, manufacturing data and information contained in submissions to regulatory authorities, whether or not protected by Intellectual Property Rights or any applications for such rights.

"Effective Date" means the date of the last Party to sign this Agreement.

"Principal Investigator" means the person who will take primary responsibility for the conduct of the Study at the Trial Site or any other person as may be agreed from time to time between the Parties as a replacement.

"Protocol" means the clinical protocol entitled "XXX" as may be modified from time to time by the Sponsor and approved by the Institutional review board and applicable regulatory authorities.

"Institution" means any public, private, entity or agency or medical facility where clinical investigations are conducted.

"Sponsor" means a legal entity which takes responsibility for the initiation, management, and financing of the Study.

"Study" means the clinical trial investigation that is to be performed in accordance with this Agreement and the Protocol for purposes of gathering information about the compound identified in the Protocol "Study Data" means data, results, information, documents, discoveries, inventions, processes and methods (whether patentable or not) resulting from or developed by Principal Investigator and/or the Institution, its employees and/or collaborators in the performance of the Study; but excluding all subject medical records.

"Study Drug" means the investigational medicinal product or control material as defined in the Protocol.

"Study Personnel"—includes, but not limited to, sub-investigators and any researchers, scientists, technicians, and other individuals employed by the Institution or any subcontractors, agents, consultants, or Affiliates of the Institution, engaged in any aspect of the Study.

"Study Subject" means a person recruited to participate in the Study.

"Trial Site" means any premises approved by the Institution and the Sponsor in which the Study will be conducted.

APPENDIX C

Rest of World (ROW) General CTA Country Requirements

Australia

- Medicines Australia template is needed.
- Local sponsor is required.

For more information on the requirements for conducting a clinical trial in Australia along with CTA requirements, go to https://www.australianclinicaltrials.gov.au/clinical-trials-toolkit#overlay-context=home.

Brazil

The sponsor or the CRO must sign an agreement or contract with the participating institution(s) and the investigator. If a sponsor decides to engage a CRO to conduct the trial, a letter of agreement should also be submitted to the authorizing bodies in the country. Parallel regulatory and ethical review is permitted. [22]

For more information on the requirements for conducting a clinical trial in Brazil along with CTA requirements, go to https://clinregs.niaid.nih.gov/single_country.php?c_id=30#trial_initiation.

---

[22] National Institute of Allergy and Infectious Diseases. Accessed November 27, 2017. https://clinregs.niaid.nih.gov/single_country.php?c_id=199

Canada

Prior to initiating the trial in Canada, the sponsor must sign an agreement between all involved parties—including ECs, qualified investigators (QIs), contract research organizations, and others—to ensure full compliance with the regulatory requirements. In-country sponsor presence or representation is required.[22]

For more information on the requirements for conducting a clinical trial in Canada along with CTA requirements, go to https://clinregs.niaid.nih.gov/single_country.php?c_id=30#trial_initiation.

China

As delineated in the PDR, the sponsor must sign an agreement or contract with the participating institution(s). The PRC-GCPs also states that, before the trial begins, the sponsor and the investigator must sign a written agreement regarding the trial protocol, monitoring, auditing, and standard operating procedures, as well as each party's responsibilities during the trial.[22]

For more information on the requirements for conducting a clinical trial in China along with CTA requirements, go to https://clinregs.niaid.nih.gov/single_country.php?c_id=30#trial_initiation.

Eastern European Countries

- Bilingual contracts are needed.
- Multiple contracts (separate PI and institution and often study team agreements, etc.) are needed.
- Large hospitals are very process/procedural driven and therefore can take a significant amount of time to negotiate simply due to the procedural requirements.
- Negotiations with private sites are quick.
- EU sponsor is required.

France

- Country template (including budget tool) is needed.
- Need to consider an incentive fee.
- Sites require numerous documents, and some sites will not start the review until all documents are received (which is important to be aware of when choosing your lead site/NC).
- EU sponsor is required.

India

As delineated in the IN-GCPs, before the trial begins, the sponsor or the CRO must sign a formal legal agreement or contract with each participating institution. If no institutions are involved, the individual investigator signature is required. The contract should define the relationship between the sponsor and the investigator/institution in terms of financial support, fees, honorarium, and payments in kind.[23]

The sponsor or the CRO must also agree to

- conduct the trial in compliance with the IN-GCPs, the applicable regulatory requirements, and the clinical trial protocol agreed to by the sponsor and approved by the EC;
- comply with the procedures for data recording and reporting;
- retain the trial-related essential documents until he or she informs the investigator(s)/institution(s) in writing that these documents are no longer needed;
- permit clinical trial-site inspections by DCGI authorized officers, as per the IN-GCPs and the DCR-2ndAmdmt; and
- in-country sponsor presence or representation is required.[23]

For more information on the requirements for conducting a clinical trial in India along with CTA requirements, go to https://clinregs.niaid.nih.gov/single_country.php?c_id=30#trial_initiation.

---

[23] National Institute of Allergy and Infectious Diseases. Accessed November 27, 2017. https://clinregs.niaid.nih.gov/single_country.php?c_id=199

Italy

- Site's contract template is needed. Nearly all are negotiable.
- Generally, contracts are in Italian only (occasionally an English template is provided for information purposes only).
- Site will not sign until after LEC approval.
- EU sponsor is required.

Kenya

Prior to initiating the trial, the G-KenyaCT requires the sponsor to sign and date an agreement with the investigator(s)/institution(s) as part of the protocol submitted for the PPB's approval or in a separate agreement.[24]

For more information on the requirements for conducting a clinical trial in Kenya along with CTA requirements, go to https://clinregs.niaid.nih.gov/single_country.php?c_id=30#trial_initiation.

Liberia

A signed clinical trial agreement is not an official requirement for Liberia. However, the G-LibClinTrial states that before the trial begins, the sponsor or his or her representative, the national PI, and the national coordinator (for a multicenter study) should sign a declaration confirming that the application is complete and accurate.[24]

For more information on the requirements for conducting a clinical trial in Liberia along with CTA requirements, go to https://clinregs.niaid.nih.gov/single_country.php?c_id=30#trial_initiation.

Malawi

The G-CTAProcsVacBiol requires the sponsor to sign a letter of agreement with the participating institutions before the clinical trial begins. In addition, the investigators and the sponsor or his or her contract research

---

[24] National Institute of Allergy and Infectious Diseases. Accessed November 27, 2017. https://clinregs.niaid.nih.gov/single_country.php?c_id=199

organization must sign an agreement specific to the clinical trial. In-country sponsor presence or representation required.[24]

For more information on the requirements for conducting a clinical trial in Malawi along with CTA requirements, go to https://clinregs.niaid.nih.gov/single_country.php?c_id=30#trial_initiation.

Peru

The sponsor and principal investigator (PI) must sign an affidavit on the preparation of the research center where the clinical trial will be executed. The sponsor must also sign an affidavit indicating that he or she will fulfill the responsibilities delineated in Decree No. 021-2017-SA. The PI must also sign an affidavit indicating his or her compliance with obligations and requirements in this regulation. Both the sponsor and the PI must sign an affidavit establishing that there is no conflict of financial interest in executing the trial. In-country sponsor presence or representation is required.[25]

For more information on the requirements for conducting a clinical trial in Peru along with CTA requirements, go to https://clinregs.niaid.nih.gov/single_country.php?c_id=30#trial_initiation.

Sierra Leone

While a signed clinical trial agreement is not an official requirement, the G-SLClinTrial states that the clinical protocol to be submitted to the PBSL must include a contractual agreement between the sponsor and the investigator.[25]

For more information on the requirements for conducting a clinical trial in Sierra Leone along with CTA requirements, go to https://clinregs.niaid.nih.gov/single_country.php?c_id=30#trial_initiation.

South Africa

According to the SA-GCPs, before the trial begins, a sponsor must prepare a written agreement that includes any information not covered in the

---

[25] National Institute of Allergy and Infectious Diseases. Accessed November 27, 2017. https://clinregs.niaid.nih.gov/single_country.php?c_id=199

protocol. The agreement must be signed by the sponsor, the PI, and any other parties involved with the trial to confirm the contract terms.[25] The sponsor should also obtain the investigator's agreement to

- conduct the trial in compliance with the SA-GCPs, the MCC requirements, and with the EC-approved protocol;
- comply with data recording/reporting procedures;
- permit monitoring, auditing, and inspection; and
- retain the trial-related essential documents until the sponsor informs the investigator(s) and institution(s) that these documents are no longer needed.
- The financial considerations of the trial should also be documented in the agreement. A declaration must be signed by the sponsor and PI stating that sufficient funds are available to complete the clinical study.[25]
- For more information on the requirements for conducting a clinical trial in South Africa along with CTA requirements, go to https://clinregs.niaid.nih.gov/single_country.php?c_id=30#trial_initiation.

Spain

- Site's contract template is needed (when working with public hospitals).
- The majority of templates are negotiable, but there are a few exceptions to the rule. For example, Madrid sites generally refuse any revisions.
- Contractual language is a mix of Spanish only, English only, or bilingual.
- Budgets should be identical, and if not identical, wording should be included in the budget submitted to the EC stating this.
- Sites will usually want to see sponsor's insurance before confirming a contract can be finalized. EU sponsor is required.

Tanzania

Prior to the trial's commencement, the protocol must be dated and signed by the investigator, the host institution, and the sponsor—and it can function as a contract. A clinical trial agreement must also be signed by the chief executive of the host institution, the sponsor, and the PI.[26]

For more information on the requirements for conducting a clinical trial in Tanzania along with CTA requirements, go to https://clinregs.niaid.nih.gov/single_country.php?c_id=30#trial_initiation.

Thailand

The G-ResEthics requires the sponsor to sign a letter of agreement with the participating institution(s) before the trial begin.[26]

For more information on the requirements for conducting a clinical trial in Thailand along with CTA requirements, go to https://clinregs.niaid.nih.gov/single_country.php?c_id=30#trial_initiation.

Uganda

Before the study begins, the sponsor must sign a formal legal agreement or contract with the participating institution. If the sponsor or PI decides to use a contract research organization to conduct the trial, a letter of agreement should also be submitted to the NDA.[26]

For more information on the requirements for conducting a clinical trial in Uganda along with CTA requirements, go to https://clinregs.niaid.nih.gov/single_country.php?c_id=30#trial_initiation.

United Kingdom

- ABPI template is needed with public hospitals (not private hospitals).
- The UK budget tool should be used when negotiating with public hospitals.

---

[26] National Institute of Allergy and Infectious Diseases. Accessed November 27, 2017. https://clinregs.niaid.nih.gov/single_country.php?c_id=199

- Many sites (but not all) will not want to start negotiations until all submissions have been performed.
- The sponsor or his or her designated representative is required to sign a letter of agreement with the participating institution before the trial begins. In addition, the investigators and the sponsor or his or her designated representative must sign an agreement specific to the clinical trial. In-country sponsor or representation is required.[27]

For more information on the requirements for conducting a clinical trial in the UK along with CTA requirements, go to https://clinregs.niaid.nih.gov/single_country.php?c_id=30#trial_initiation.

Vietnam

After obtaining a copy of the EECBR approval, the sponsor is required to sign a letter of agreement with the participating host institution before the trial begins. The sponsor is also required to sign a clinical trial contract with the principal investigator.

For more information on the requirements for conducting a clinical trial in the Vietnam along with CTA requirements, go to https://clinregs.niaid.nih.gov/single_country.php?c_id=30#trial_initiation.

Some of the information contained in this section was obtained from clinregs.niaid.nih.gov, which you can visit for much more information on conducting clinical trials in various countries. Also, a big thank you to TCS (CRO) LTD. for sharing some of their insights (www.tcs-cro.com).

---

[27] National Institute of Allergy and Infectious Diseases. Accessed November 27, 2017. https://clinregs.niaid.nih.gov/single_country.php?c_id=199

ABOUT THE AUTHOR

Débora S. Araujo has over a decade of experience in the pharmaceutical industry, working and consulting for Fortune 500 companies. During her time in this industry, her special focus has been on the business aspects of clinical trials. She has utilized her expertise and knowledge to drive practical change in this industry via thought leadership material, conference presentations, and other engagements.

Most recently, Débora's passion for driving practical change along with her forward-thinking bent led her to launch ClinBiz (www.clinbiz.com), an online platform with a dedicated YouTube channel, podcast, blog and much more where clinical research professionals can stay connected and updated on the latest topics, trends and technologies related to the business aspects of clinical trials.

When she is not contributing in the business world, Débora loves to spend time relaxing with her husband, Altair, and her two boys, Matthew and Timothy, in the great garden state of New Jersey.

Made in the USA
Columbia, SC
11 July 2025